Dr. Alicia Holland's

EXPANDING
Your
Tutoring Business:
The Blueprint for Building
a Global Learning Organization
2nd Edition

Book Titles by Dr. Alicia Holland

Dr. Holland-Johnson's
Becoming a Better Tutor:
A Data-Driven Approach to Tutoring (2ⁿᵈ Edition)

Book 1:
Dr. Holland-Johnson's
Expanding Your Tutoring Business:
*The Blueprint for Building a Global Learning Organization
(1ˢᵗ and 2ⁿᵈ Editions)*

Book 2:
Dr. Holland-Johnson's
Expanding Your Tutoring Business:
The Blueprint for Hiring Tutors and Independent Contractors

Book 3:
Dr. Holland-Johnson's
Expanding Your Tutoring Business:
The Blueprint for Protecting Your Learning Organization

Book 4:
Dr. Holland-Johnson's
Expanding Your Tutoring Business:
*The Blueprint for Evaluating Tutors and Implementing
Professional Development For Your Learning Organization*

Dr. Holland-Johnson's
Starting and Operating an Online Tutoring Business:
The Blueprint for Running an Online Learning Organization

Note: Check Dr. Holland's Personal Website for her latest work at
www.dr-holland.com

Dr. Alicia Holland's

EXPANDING
Your
Tutoring Business:
The Blueprint for Building
a Global Learning Organization
2nd Edition

Dr. Alicia Holland, EdD

This book may be ordered through booksellers or by contacting:

iGlobal Educational Services, LLC
13785 Highway 183, Suite 125
Austin, Texas 78750
www.iglobaleducation.com
512-761-5898

Because of the dynamic nature of the Internet, any web addresses or links contained in this book may have changed since publication and may no longer be valid. The views expressed in this work are solely those of the author and do not necessarily reflect the views of the publisher, and the publisher hereby disclaims any responsibility for them.

Dr. Alicia Holland's Expanding Your Tutoring Business: The Blueprint for Building a Global Learning Organization.

ISBN-13: 978-1-944346-45-4

Book Titles by **Dr. Holland**
(also professionally known as Dr. Holland-Johnson)

Dedication

This book is dedicated to those who are seeking to make a different in their clients' lives both academically and personally. This profession requires bold and selfless individuals to share their knowledge with the rest of the world while serving as a merchant of hope to individuals who need help with their learning needs.

Georgia, Amaiya, and future children, this book is also dedicated to each of you and to your future success.

Table of Contents

CHAPTER 8: Giving Back to the Community

How This Book is Organized

D r. Alicia Holland's *Expanding Your Tutoring Business: The Blue Print for Building a Global Learning Organization* is organized by chapters—the following sections explain what you will find in each chapter.

Chapter 1: Becoming a Legitimate Tutoring Company

In this chapter, I discuss all of the steps necessary to get your tutoring company legitimate so that you can do business. You will have an opportunity to assess your start-up needs and learn how to properly budget for projects that will need to be done for your business. In addition, I talk about the importance of selecting a business name, logo, and corporate identity package that will promote your company's brand.

Chapter 2: Selecting the Right Office Environment for Your Tutoring Clients

Once you have decided upon a business name and took some time to look at a proper budget for your tutoring organization, it is time to choose the best office environment for your tutoring business. Whether you are meeting with clients or want an office that you can concentrate on business activities, you still need to have some guidelines on how to find the best office space and how to snag the best office lease deal. In this chapter, you will have the opportunity to assess your office needs, identify the must-have office items and security features, and determine a budget for your office needs and furniture.

Chapter 3: Assessing Your Human Resources (HR) Needs

In Chapter 3, you will assess your HR Needs and learn how to develop your own organizational structure. Most importantly, you will have the time to carefully plan key positions and develop job descriptions and pay structures that will attract talent to work at your learning organization. Last but not least, you will also learn about setting budgets for projects and analyze when it is appropriate to outsource and what to avoid when using this method for company projects.

Chapter 4: Corporate Meetings and Minutes for Your Tutoring Business

You are in the big leagues now and there is a lot of paperwork that goes with it. In Chapter 4, you will learn the importance of holding corporate meetings and how to prepare for your first meeting. In addition, you will have the opportunity to develop a meeting schedule and determine the types of information that goes into corporate minutes. Last but not least, you will have an opportunity to carefully plan a system to help organize corporate meetings, bylaws, and other important information related to your learning organization.

Chapter 5: Planning Orientations for Your Learning Organization

In Chapter 5, I discuss the importance of orientations for your tutoring business and take you on a journey of identifying and describing the various types of orientations in which you will need to work with your clients and tutors. Lastly, you will have an opportunity to learn how to select the best platform for delivering orientations within your learning organization.

Chapter 6: Developing Handbooks for Your Learning Organization

Everyone in the learning organization needs to know what to do. In Chapter 6, you will identify your handbook needs for your learning organization and develop a strategic plan for writing handbooks. Additionally, you will have an opportunity to describe the various types of handbooks in which you might need, along with understanding the importance of copyrighting your handbooks.

Chapter 7: Listening to the People Who Matters

In Chapter 7, you will focus on the value of surveys, reviews, and customer feedback. This chapter affords you the chance to take the time out to identify and describe various types of surveys that you may need in your very own learning organization. So, take heed to the people who matters the most and you will discover who they are in this chapter.

Chapter 8: Giving Back to the Community

Chapter 8 is packed with strategies on how to get out and serve your community, along with giving back to your community. In this chapter, you will have a chance to identify both the Merchants of Hopes in your life and exactly what are your communities. Additionally, you will learn how to develop your own scholarship and volunteer program to give others a chance.

Introduction

This book is part one of four in the *Expanding Your Tutoring Business* Series. It is conceived and created for the independent tutor and courageous educator who desire to take their tutoring business to the next level. My seminal work on tutoring Becoming a Better Tutor: A Data-Driven Approach to Tutoring, has been well received since its first publication in 2010.

This is my first comprehensive book series on tutoring; that is, it serves as the blueprint for individuals to step up their game from a home-based tutoring business to a full-fledged global learning organization that offers tutoring and so much more to clients around the world.

I'm a certified teacher, professional tutor, instructional designer, curriculum developer, online professor, educational consultant, researcher and global business owner. I've stepped out on faith to follow my lifelong passion and dream. The information presented in this series is based on insight and actual experiences that I have encountered over the years in building my own global learning organization.

This book series will help you build a solid and successful global learning organization. You'll find advice herein on how to position your learning organization to prosper in such an ever-changing global market. Whether you are a new tutor or veteran tutor, I will show you how to do what you love full-time—helping others learn and grow and sharing your knowledge with the world. My ultimate goal within my professional career and this book series is to inspire and transform others according to their life purpose. But first, you have to believe in yourself and your potential. Now is the time to begin!

Acknowledgments

I cannot say this enough, but I must give glory to God for helping me realize my potential and purpose in life. Thanks to my editor, Jena Roach, who has helped build confidence in my writing skills and challenged me to expand my ideas.

My Assumptions

In order to provide you with material to meet your unique situation, I had to make some basic assumptions about your tutoring business. I assume the following:

1. You have a genuine interest in the tutoring industry.
2. You want information on how to build a global learning organization to help individuals around the globe.
3. You are ready to start or expand your tutoring business.

CHAPTER 1

Becoming A Legitimate Tutoring Company

"If you are planning for a year, sow rice, if you are planning for a decade, plant trees; if you are planning for a lifetime, educate people".

—*Chinese Proverb*

U p to this point, you have probably been doing business under an assumed name, which is fine. Are you ready to take your tutoring business to the next level? Before you can file for a business, you must create a vision and mission statement to help with selecting a business name and other identity for your tutoring business.

Creating a Vision and Mission Statement

You probably already have both a vision and mission statement in mind. If you are already running a home-based tutoring business, then you want to examine these statements to gain inspiration so that you can move your tutoring business forward.

Here are three powerful questions to help you create your vision and mission statement:

1. How many target market(s) do you plan to serve? Identify them.

   _____
   _____
   _____
   _____
   _____

2. What is the purpose of your learning organization?

   _____
   _____
   _____
   _____
   _____

3. How do you plan to serve your clients?

   _____
   _____
   _____
   _____
   _____

Expert's Advice:

You may already know these answers, or you may need to see the logo before putting your vision on paper. Thus, I think that you should do what naturally fits.

Selecting a Business Name

Your business name will be how people recognize your services and products. In the business world, this is called branding. You want to make your business stand out so others will know that you are unique. As a business owner, you can be extremely creative or simple with your business name.

Select a business name that embodies both your vision and mission statement. Make it unique. In other words, choose wisely.

Please write down your answers to the following questions. Your responses will guide you in making the right choice about selecting a business name for your learning organization.

1. What does your business stand for?

_____

_____

_____

_____

_____

2. When potential clients look at your business name, what would you like for them to see? Name at least seven adjectives.

_____

_____

_____

_____

_____

Adjective List:

_____

_____

_____

_____

_____

3. How would your business name define all the services and products?

_____

_____

_____

_____

_____

4. Will your business name survive growth? Why or why not? Will the name of your company transition with future growth?

_____

_____

_____

_____

_____

5. List at least three potential business names, along with taglines, to represent the services and products offered.

_____

_____

_____

_____

_____

6. Ask trusted individuals which business name sounds professional. How did they respond?

_____

_____

_____

_____

_____

7. What is your intuition telling you about your potential
business name?

_____

_____

_____

_____

_____

Expert's Advice:

Selecting the business name is the most important aspect of building a global learning organization. I know firsthand how selecting the right business name impacts the future and direction your organization will take.

When I started out locally as a private tutor, I was doing business as Realistic Measures & Consulting. At that time, my private home-based tutoring business was focusing on realistic results according to the student's learning needs. Thus, my tagline was "Believe in Yourself and Go Far"™.

After expanding my tutoring business into a learning organization, the business structure changed. It was the perfect time to reevaluate a new business name. In March 2011, iGlobal Educational Services was born.

iGlobal Educational Services was selected because our vision is to serve a global market, for which we are currently providing. While I still have the personal belief of "Believe in Yourself and Go Far". I kept my organization's new motto under this theme. iGlobal Educational Services' tagline is the following: "Believe. Inspire. Transform."™ It represents the past, present, and future of how my tutoring business has evolved into a great learning organization to help others.

Filing for a Business Structure

There are many business structures available to consider. You must visit your accountant or seek a free consultation to fully understand the options. Most tutoring companies are formed as Limited Liability Companies (LLC). However, there are other choices to choose from, which are outlined below:

Sole Proprietor	Limited Liability Company	Partnership
Working as an independent contractor.	Owned by one or more individuals. Members can function as a corporation. Working as a company and hiring employees and/or independent contractors.	Owned by two individuals. Working as a company and hiring employees and/or independent contractors.

Scenario: "Merry-Go Round"

Destiny Purpose, a well-sought reading tutor in her community, anticipated an additional annual income of $5,000 just from her part-time tutoring. She operated her tutoring business as a sole proprietor and took on the assumed name of

Scenario: "Merry-Go Round" (continued)

"Destiny's Tutoring Services." At the end of the tax year, she tallied all expenses related to her home-based business and quickly realized that she had spent over $1,000 and earned $5,000 in additional income.

For the past two years, she had been doing her own taxes using the online tax software. When she entered the required information, she was shocked to learn that she had to pay money to the Internal Revenue Service (IRS). That very next day, she called a local accountant and scheduled a free consultation. The accountant explained that those numbers were very likely because of her business structure, which was a sole proprietorship. Thus, the accountant recommended that she formed a LLC due to her specific tax information.

This business structure change would open up the door for promptly deducting business expenses and other perks. However, more paperwork is involved such as accounting, payroll and taxes, annual meetings with published minutes, and other required documentation. The accountant did say that a new business name would have to be established. Destiny was devastated because she knew how hard it would be to start over. However, she kept a positive attitude and thanked the accountant.

Expert's Advice:

Knowledge is power. It was wise to contact this accountant because she was able to learn that she now needed to legalize her business as a corporation, a sub-chapter corporation for LLCs.

From a business perspective, this is incredibly significant.

Destiny started out as a sole proprietor to build her clientele and demand for her tutoring services. When it came time to take her business to the next level, she was able to do so. Since this is very new to her, I would recommend that Destiny continue to take steps to educate herself. This will help her build a dynamic learning organization.

Where to Look for Help

After deciding on a business structure and submitting the necessary legal paperwork, it is time to get some additional business insight. Did you know that there are organizations that are willing to help entrepreneurs, like yourself, start a new business?

Here are some places to help you get started:

1. SCORE
2. The Small Business Administration (SBA)
3. Publications [i.e. www.entrepreneur.com and www.becomingabettertutor.com]
4. Local University Small Business Development Center
5. City and State Resources

Selecting a Logo and Corporate Identity Package

This is one of the fun parts of starting a business! You will need to select a logo to set yourself apart from your competition. It is best to get a corporate identity package that includes a logo design, business card, and other design of your choice. However, if you are on a budget, try to get the logo first.

A typical corporate identity package will include the following items:

Typical Corporate Identity Package	
Item	**Purpose**
Logo Design	Sets your business apart from others. It's your brand name for your services and products.
Letterhead	Identifies communication from the company. This can be created by using only the logo files.
Business Card	Informs potential clients that you're in business. This is an absolute necessity for your tutoring business.
Post Card	Drives traffic to your tutoring business.
Presentation Folder	Shows professionalism with tutoring services.
Brochure Design	Showcases all services and products to potential clients.
Flyer	Drives traffic to your tutoring business.

Each of these marketing materials is very important. However, a priority list can be created based upon your tutoring business's needs.

Expert's Advice:

From my own personal experience, I started out with the basic corporate identity package. This included a logo and business card design. Typically logo designs can be saved in various formats, which results in saving money for a letterhead design.

Another necessity was a website. When I asked clients how they found me, the number one response was always online. Therefore,

I made more investments in my website design and utilized other marketing strategies.

Assessing Start-Up Needs and Budget

If you are already in business, then this may be a breeze for you because you got everything that you already need, or so you think.

When starting a corporation, individuals will quickly learn that there are requirements that must be in place before getting an office space in a commercial setting or even taking on state and federal contracts.

Below is a list of items that you will need to budget:

1. Office Supplies
2. Office Space
3. Software
4. Marketing Materials
5. Payroll and Taxes
6. Office Technology
7. Business Insurances
8. Outsourcing
9. Travel
10. Professional Development

Let's take a look at the various types of items that will need to be budgeted and why they are important to helping your tutoring business flourish.

Office Supplies Budget

The first item that will need to be budgeted is office supplies. This includes technology, software, and furniture.

Office Supplies

Common office supplies that will be used regularly are listed below:

- Presentation folders
- File folders
- Label Maker
- Pens and Pencils
- Clipboard
- Boxes
- Jump drives
- CDs (recordable)
- Highlighters
- White-out
- Permanent markers
- Paper clips
- Color paper
- Envelopes (all sizes)
- Binder clips
- All-purpose copy paper
- Stapler (Heavy duty)

Office Technology

Common office technologies that will be used regularly are listed below:

- Fax machine
- Copier (Laser)
- iPad
- Lots of Ink and Toner
- Computers (Desktop and Laptop)
- Microphone Headset

- Phone Line
- Printer

Software

Common software for the office that will be used regularly is listed below:

- Microsoft Professional Office
- Adobe Creative Suite
- LiveScribe Pen
- My Attorney Software

Office Furniture

Common furniture for the office that will be used regularly is listed below:

- Bookcases
- Chairs and tables
- Conference table
- Receptionist desk
- Office desks
- Trash cans
- Filing cabinets (Secured)

In addition to these , you need to budget for miscellaneous items such as décor. While this budget does not have to be huge, careful consideration should be used when trying to decorate your office to create a positive business environment.

Even if your business is online, you still need to have your office decorated whether it is seasonal or year-round. This puts you in a professional frame of mind to complete your best work. Not to mention, if you do have clients who occasionally meet with you face-to-face, they will see that you are no amateur and conduct business as a professional.

Office Space Budget

The next item that you should budget for is office space. (See Chapter 2 for how to assess your office space needs.)

Whether you desire to work from home or at an alternative location, you will still need a place to do your work free of distractions and wandering eyes. When you are working with intellectual property you must protect it, even at your home.

Expert's Advice:

You may not think about it if you are working out of your home, but you need to save money now. As a sole proprietor, it may be so tempting to take and spend every dollar…and in some cases, you have to cover certain expenses. Thus, the goal is to save 25% of each project towards rent.

For instance, let's say that you made $1,000 per month for tutoring services.

From that, 10% of $1,000 is $100 while 5% of $1,000 is $50. Thus, when that amount is added, we have 25% of $1,000 is $250.

Based upon this example, this tutor should be saving $250 if he or she makes $1,000. In other words, individuals should be saving 25% of each project toward rent expenses that are incurred monthly.

I highly recommend reading and completing the exercises in Chapter 2 of this book before setting an office space budget. This will provide better insight into your tutoring business's needs and will help you plan appropriately.

Marketing Budget

The third item that you need to budget is marketing materials. While you may have a huge list ready to try to promote your tutoring business, it is best to choose your marketing strategies wisely. In my first tutoring book, *Becoming a Better Tutor: A Data-Driven Approach to Tutoring*, I mention that there are two types of marketing strategies. These include both basic and advanced marketing strategies.

Below is a table of each type of strategies listed under the appropriate marketing category:

Basic Marketing Strategies	Advanced Marketing Strategies
Online Advertising	Offering Sponsorships
Local Advertising	Website
Networking	Direct mailing and Newsletters
	Joining your Local Chamber of Commerce

(Alicia Holland, 2010, pp. 28-29)

In addition to these listed strategies, individuals should be using more advanced strategies to connect with new and existing clients.

Don't assume that because your business is expanding, you also have to expand your marketing budget. This is not the case, though extra funds are beneficial when applying to those advanced marketing strategies such as press releases.

Payroll and Taxes Budget

The fourth item you will need to budget for is payroll and taxes. It is expected that employers set up an account with the state workforce agency. If you have hired a payroll company to help you with these needs, they will help manage this account when payroll is run each month. The main advantage of working with a payroll company is that they are held responsible. In fact, if there is an error on their behalf, they will pay for it.

Common tax reporting includes the following:

1. **Sales and Use Tax**
2. **Franchise Tax**

These types of taxes can be filed by you. When it comes time to start paying yourself, then you will need to start looking for experienced and trustworthy payroll companies that are both cost-effective and provide exceptional customer service. When hiring a company to do payroll and taxes, you should look for businesses that can provide full-service payroll and tax filings. It would not hurt to see if it also offers additional human resource services.

Expert's Advice:

You may think that it is not important to do payroll and taxes. This is only true if you are working as a sole proprietor because you get to keep what you make.

As a learning organization, it is very important to begin running payroll and reporting taxes. There are many organizations, including software that can calculate payroll and taxes. Depending on the state in which you are conducting business, there are certain requirements such as sales tax and franchise tax reporting.

When it comes to taxes at either the state or federal levels, it is best that you contact these tax agencies on your own. For example, Texas business owners would contact the state comptroller's office regarding any questions related to sales and tax use. When it comes to federal taxes, the best point of contact is the Internet Revenue Services (IRS).

Whether you decide to sell products or not, you are still required to apply for sales permit that lists your place of business.

When I expanded my tutoring business, all these taxes were very new to me. I quickly learned that I had made the best decision to start out as a home-based tutoring business. I searched online for local business courses for small business owners and was very blessed to find a workshop related to taxes.

I was proud to pay $35 to attend this workshop because it helped me start out on the right road with business tax obligations.

Business Insurance Budget

The fifth item is to seek business insurance. If you get your own lease agreement, you will need business insurance prior to moving into the office space. Depending on your organizational structure, you will need (at the minimum) the following types of business insurances.

- **Professional Liability**

This type of insurance protects professional advice and service companies from negligence claims. For example, if you find yourself in a situation that may involve damages or other issues, then this will cover you and your business.

- **Automobile Insurance**

If your business has vehicles that are used by tutors or to transport students, it is required to have this type of insurance. If your business does not have any vehicles for business use, then it is in your business's best interest to provide a written explanation when submitting bids to complete various projects. This is only if the project requires showing proof of business insurances and coverage.

Worker's Compensation Liability Insurance

This is another type of insurance that is needed to be in business. It covers any accidents on the job. Most state and federal contracts require worker's compensation liability insurance.

Outsourcing Budget

The sixth item that needs to be budgeted is to outsource projects. There will be some projects that you will not have time to do or know how to do. Therefore, it is very important to outsource projects. For example, these projects can range from accounting, writing, lead generation, and so forth.

Expert's Advice:

Don't enter into outsourcing thinking that you do not have to check on the contractor. In reality, you will have to lead them in order to get the desired outcome. Otherwise, you will become bitter and disappointed. You must understand what you want and provide written instructions.

Travel Budget

The seventh item is a travel budget. You will need to budget for travel, even if you work online. It is expected that you will attend professional development opportunities such as conferences or other informative opportunities. You may also need to budget for business trips that may be outside of your geographical area.

Items that should be budgeted are the following:
- Gas
- Hotel
- Meals
- Toll fees
- Air fare and associated fees
- Bus fare
- Taxi fare
- Rentals

Professional Development Budget

The last item is professional development. Let's face it, no one knows everything. That's why we take courses to further our knowledge base. Specifically, in your tutoring business, there will be many things that you will need to learn to stay competitive in such a global economy.

Below are some recommended business courses to help you be successful with your tutoring business:

1. QuickBooks
2. Intellectual Property
3. Tax Requirement
4. Record-Keeping
5. Leadership
6. Customer Service
7. Social Media Marketing

While many conferences are offered throughout the year, it is very important to carefully select which ones you will attend. Traveling to conferences can be costly, but you get to see some very exciting places and meet different people from many walks of life.

You have been presented with good information that can help you begin to think about how you want to birth your learning organization. Proper planning and assessment of your tutoring business needs will lead you to a greater chance of success with your organization.

CHAPTER 2

Selecting the Right Office Environment for Your Tutoring Clients

"Once you make a decision, the universe conspires to make it happen."

—*Ralph Waldo Emerson*

A t this point, you may be ready to move your tutoring practice to a professional office setting. Please keep in mind that this is primarily a mental transition. In other words, you were already operating a professional business at home, but it's time to take it up a notch and move your business forward by getting the office space like the rest of the professional world. Have you ever been in a crowded or old-fashioned office? How did it may you feel? Prior to finding an office space, I highly suggest reflecting on your own experiences in offices and build a schema of how you would want your clients to feel. Sometimes, your office space has a lot to do with whether clients will come back to receive tutoring services.

Assessing Your Office Needs

Let's look at assessing your office needs. Before you can get an office, you need to answer a few questions so you can become aware of what you really want from your office space.

Please write down your answers to the following questions:

1. How many clients are you currently serving? How do you keep track of this number?

_____

_____

_____

_____

_____

2. Why do you need an office space?

_____

_____

_____

_____

_____

3. How many employees do you plan on hiring? If none, at what point in your business do you foresee hiring additional individuals?

_____

_____

_____

_____

_____

4. What are your future plans with your business?

_____

_____

_____

_____

_____

5. Will this office space grow into your needs? How do you know?

_____

_____

_____

_____

_____

6   What is your budget for office space? Does it include utilities?

_____

_____

_____

_____

_____

7. Do you have a backup plan in case the office space arrangement does not work out? Why or why not? Describe it.

_____

_____

_____

_____

8. If you have extra office space, how will you use it? Will you rent it out to other beginning professionals?

_____

_____

_____

_____

_____

9. Could your tutoring business run solely with a virtual office? Why or why not?

_____

_____

_____

_____

_____

Your responses to these questions will guide you in determining how much office space is needed, if any. Also, they will help you discover how much money you'll need to budget to find a quality office space and furnish it.

Expert's Advice:

You will need a professional office space for two reasons: (1) You need a stable place to do business; and (2) You need to build credibility for your business.

I used to think that working out of my home was great—and it truly is when your tutoring business is either online, or you don't have to meet with clients on a regular basis. However, when family and friends visit, they may begin to ask a great deal of questions about the business based upon what they see. It is very important to keep business information proprietary so that you can stay in business.

Now that you have assessed your office space needs, it is time to figure out how you want to receive business mail.

Figuring Out How to Receive Business Mail

There are plenty of options to receive business mail. We are going to look at four.

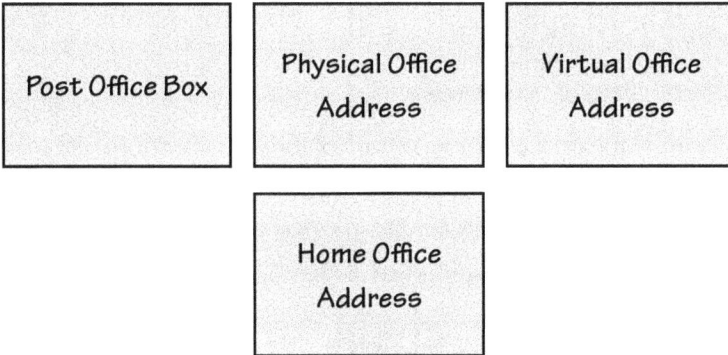

Post Office Box	Physical Office Address	Virtual Office Address

Home Office Address

Option 1: Post Office Box

The first option to receive mail is to get a Post Office (P.O.) Box. This type of address allows stability and the fastest way to get mail each day. Please keep in mind that some work contracts, such as government contracts, will require individuals to also have a physical address for deliveries, such as packages and overnight mail.

Option 2: Physical Office Address

The second option to receive mail is to get a physical office address. The type of lease agreement one signs will determine whether or not tenants can receive mail at that location. There's nothing wrong with using your office address because you are a legitimate business. To avoid any discrepancies, it is wise to also have a physical office address that is located at an actual business office complex.

Option 3: Virtual Office Address

The third option to receive mail is to get a virtual office address. This is a virtual office, which means you do not have to be physically located there.

Depending on your office needs, you may opt to get a virtual office that will allow you to meet at their location for a specific time or other purposes.

Option 4: Home Office Address

The fourth option to receive mail is to get a home office. This is the easiest way to get things shipped to you without the hassle of driving in traffic, spending extra money on postage, or having the risk of someone else taking your mail without your knowledge.

Determining how to take on an office lease agreement

When it comes time to look for office space, you need to understand that there are two types of office lease agreements that you will encounter for your tutoring business.

Month-to-Month Lease Agreement

The first type of lease agreement is exactly what it states, a monthly rent payment. If you are a start-up company, it is best to get one of these after your term lease is up. After the lease is up, it goes on to month-to-month. Typically, landlords only offer three- , six- , or nine-month leases.

Term Lease Agreement

The second type of lease agreement is a term lease. This type of lease is available for established businesses and can act as some type of security.

Whether your business is new or established, you must also focus on your business plan and office needs. Ask yourself pointed questions such as: "Where do you see your business five years from now?" You must have a plan regarding your office space. Otherwise you will get lost and waste money that you need to get yourself in business.

No matter your reason, you should always have a plan in place for your business. It's very important to visualize how you want your business.

To date, there's not one business owner who wants their business stagnant or obsolete.

Let's look at a few situations regarding office space.

Scenario 1: "Who Stole My Chips?"

Shiletha, a math tutor, started her home-based tutoring business shortly after leaving the classroom. She had a steady schedule with clients from three to seven p.m. and tutored only Mondays through Thursdays. In other words, she conducted twenty tutoring sessions per week.

Her tutoring office was upstairs and parents waited in her old formal living room next to the front entrance. Shiletha did not have issues with this type of arrangement until she witnessed one of her client's parents eat her bananas and chips. Can you imagine the look on Shiletha's face? She was livid because she had offered them water and asked if they wanted food. Shiletha continued to work with the client, but parents were not allowed in her home.

That same night, Shiletha started looking for office space to accommodate her growing tutoring business. How would you have handled this situation?

Expert's Advice:

Shiletha did the right thing by conducting tutoring sessions at her home until her business grew. This was a very smart move. However, Shiletha should have had a plan in place or procedures with parents who decide to stay while their child is being tutored.

Most parents like to drop their children off, but a policy must be in place for late-pickups and early arrivals. Policies keep everything in order and are very professional.

Shiletha should have known that her business was ready to move on from her house. Why do you think she was still conducting her tutoring sessions from her home?

Scenario 2: "Exit Gracefully"

Benzy, an all-around tutor, found a nice, shared office space in a centralized location for all his clients. He was so excited to finally be away from his house and actually feel like a professional. While he only had a single office of 300 square feet, he was still able to manage his tutoring business. His rent was only $325, which included all utilities plus free Internet. Benzy carried out his three-month lease and opted to rent on a month-to-month basis.

He began receiving mail there since he had to provide a business address for most of his transactions. He also opened his business checking account. Benzy decided that he would explore other markets and within six months, his business was booming. Other companies, including the landlord, began to question his business. They wanted to know how business was booming in such a tough economy. Soon Benzy noticed that he was not receiving his bank statements. He thought it was sent electronically and opted to have it mailed to him.

Scenario 2: "Exit Gracefully" *(continued)*

About two weeks later, Benzy received a phone call from the state's workforce agency regarding returned mail. The state's representative informed him that the mail correspondence was being returned. She also warned him that this doesn't look good for a new business. She suggested that Benzy got a PO Box to prevent this type of issue for reoccurring again.

It became so clear that the only person who could have done this was the landlord because she was the only person who had access to the mail. Benzy was irate because he would have never thought that his landlord would do this. That same day, Benzy turned in his 30-day notice with a smile and did not look back.

Expert's Advice:

Benzy did what he had to do. At the end of the day, he is responsible for his business affairs. At one point, this office was perfect for him. It's unfortunate that he had to leave an office that he loved and could afford. However, no individual should have to endure this type of office environment and spiteful behavior, especially if he or she is paying to be there.

Based upon Benzy's experience, I recommend all new businesses get a PO Box address. This will eliminate issues concerning mail and will be a great idea if you are leasing office space.

Chances are you will not permanently stay in your lease because most business owners desire to own their own office space. Therefore, a PO Box will allow you to move around according to your budget and office needs. At the very least, you will have the security of knowing that you will receive your mail. Not to mention, a PO Box is considered an office expense and it is tax deductible.

Scenario 3:
"Go Ahead and Take Over… It's Gonna Cost You"

Truth Kristina, a tutor business owner, decided that she wanted to take her business to a professional-office setting. She had operated her business by herself for five years out of her home and thought that it was time to hire other tutors. The business was financially fit and she had nothing stopping her.

She decided to look online for an office space, and she found an ad that someone had posted. It read something like this:

"Online Ad for Office Space—
It can be Yours NOW literally"

"We are looking for someone to take over our lease. We have 8 months left on the lease and will transfer our security deposit to you PLUS you can move in by the end of the month.

This is not a scam, if you are interested, call or reply back to me. This will not last… I promise you."

Truth Kristina saw this ad and thought that it was a no brainer. She applied for the office space, which was over 1,800 square feet at $1.00 per square foot. Her lease application was accepted. Truth Kristina started making plans on how she would utilize the new office space and began setting up utilities to be activated on the move-in date.

To her surprise, two weeks later, the landlord called Truth Kristina and said that she could not move in under those terms because this was not brought to his attention by the real estate company who was initiating the lease agreement. Truth Kristina later learned that the tenant had posted this ad and the real estate agent had approved. Truth Kristina was hurt because she had spent all that time planning and setting up utilities. Her plans had yet been put on hold again. She even had the money to pay the security deposit plus first month's rent, but she felt hoodwinked. Therefore, she opted to bow out and move on to the next one.

Before she let this issue go, Truth Kristina requested that her lease application fee be returned. Fortunately, the real estate company agreed and apologized for the confusion. Two days later, Truth Kristina found a virtual office, which was even better and less expensive.

Expert's Advice:

Truth Kristina did the right thing by giving up the office and let the tenant fend for himself. This battle was not for Truth Kristina and it's a good thing that she realized it before it was too late.

From a business perspective, it is always good to get at least four to five quotes on different types of office spaces. In this case, anyone with common sense like Truth Kristina would have definitely capitalized on this opportunity.

The best advice I can give you is to find your own lease agreement for your company. That way, there are no surprises. Make sure that you read your lease carefully. You will be amazed at what the fine print may say.

Scenario 4: "At last, I'm in Office Heaven"

Caleb Matthew, an online tutoring business owner, started out three years ago as a traveling private tutor who was very successful with face-to-face tutoring. This past year, he decided

Scenario 4: "At last, I'm in Office Heaven" *(continued)*

that he would try online tutoring with some of his clients. Caleb quickly learned that he could do more online and reach a broader audience, which aligned to his professional goals.

To his surprise, his clients liked it too and stopped wanting to come to his professional office or see him at their home. Therefore, Caleb Matthew announced that he only tutored students online. Shortly after, he noticed that he did not need a professional office with a great deal of expenses. He didn't know much about virtual offices, but later discovered that he should have had one. He could get a virtual office for as little as $50 per month plus a receptionist and mail forwarding. In other words, he got more bang for his buck.

He decided that he would get a virtual office and conduct his online tutoring business out of his home. He also had the option of working at the physical location of the virtual office as well.

Expert's Advice:

I am totally inspired by Caleb because he did not neglect his face-to-face clients, but rather educated them in more than two ways. He was able to work with learners around the globe. If he has a virtual business, then it makes sense to have a virtual office as well.

Please understand that there are many options available for virtual offices. However, I strongly recommend getting one that provides more than mail forwarding. For example, if you need to meet school officials or other clients, then you want to have a professional office available to reflect your legitimate global learning organization. This makes you look professional, knowledgeable, and represents your organization well.

Virtual offices are good for organizations that do not meet clients on a regular basis.

Each of these situations will definitely provide insight into what can happen when looking for office space. The best advice is to assess your office needs prior to falling in love with one so that you can know what you truly want and need.

Identifying the Must-Have Office Items and Security Features

Now that you have an office space or on the verge of sealing the deal for one, you need to know what is needed to run your tutoring business effectively. While it may seem like common sense, moving from one location to the next causes business owners to need different pieces of furniture. If this is what goes on in an established business, can you imagine what start-up businesses are experiencing?

Whether you are conducting business online or face-to-face, business owners need to make sure that they have the following:

Must-Have In The Office	
Receptionist desk	Waiting room
Desk	Whiteboard
Conference table	Secured filing cabinets
Storage area for office supplies	Magazines
Paper shredder	Copier (black and color printer)
Chairs	Décor

Each one of these items plays a major role in one's business success. Clients like to feel welcomed and secure while being tutored. Please make sure that you purchase your items with security features.

Budgeting for Your Office Needs and Furniture

Have you heard of designing on a nickel? This is something worth trying because you will quickly learn that your business requires you to get more than office furniture. Your tutoring business will need the following to get started or to be run legally:

List of Items that You Will Need to Budget for Your Tutoring Business	
Types of Budgets	**Items Covered Under Each Project**
Business Insurance	Coverage needed: Professional Liability, Automobile Insurance (if applicable), Worker's Compensation Liability
Office Space	Physical or virtual location
Marketing	Business Cards, Brochures, Postcards, Presentation folders, Press releases, Promotional products
Payroll and Taxes	Human Resources (HR) Services that takes care of payroll and taxes, and may want to consider looking to a legit company who can take care of all the HR needs for your tutoring business.
Office Expense	Office supplies, décor, printers and ink, postage
Outsourcing	All outsourced projects

Travel	Gas, hotel, food, tolls, oil change, and any other task related to business travel or use.
Professional Development	Business classes, continuing education courses, workshops, professional conferences, and other educational activities to improve skills and the business.
Technology	Any item related to technology, especially if you run an online tutoring business.

Now that you have had a chance to see what your office needs are, I highly suggest that you take some time to look at the items that you will need for your office and begin putting a plan into place. Utilizing these budgets will keep your business expenses lean while saving you money that can be used in other areas. Extra funds could lead to significant growth for your company!

CHAPTER 3

Assessing Your Human Resources (HR) Needs

"The reward of a thing well done, is to have done it."
—*Ralph Waldo Emerson*

L et's face it—you will need more than yourself to run your tutoring company. There will be a lot of demands that will be totally different and most reputable learning organizations, especially the government will be asking for a formal analysis of how you conduct business.

As a result, you need to know how to plan for staffing, create and plan budgets for various projects, and so forth. Your HR needs is another one of those lifebloods of any organization. As a result, this part of your organizational health should not be taken lightly and should be handled with care.

Assessing Your HR Needs

What is your organizational structure? You may have started out as just one individual. In this case, your tutoring business is considered an organic organization or has an organic structure because of the flexibility and fast-growing changes. On the other hand, your organizational structure should look like the following:

This organizational chart describes how you may be the only employee while the other side shows the various projects and independent contractors. Though only three projects are listed, more can be added. However, this is a realistic view of what can be expected for a small tutoring business.

Developing an Organizational Structure and Identifying Key Positions

You may have already discovered that it would be nice to have some help to manage your business. Once you have the revenue to fund more job positions, set a budget for each position. In order to set the budget, individuals must first identify the key positions necessary to run the learning organization.

Here are six questions to consider when trying identifying key positions. Each of these questions is crucial to identifying key positions for your learning organization.

1. What is your current organizational structure?

      _____
      _____
      _____
      _____
      _____

2. How do you want your projected organizational structure to look?

_____

_____

_____

_____

_____

3. In two paragraphs, describe the purpose of each key position?

_____

_____

_____

_____

_____

4. How much would you work for someone else's company doing the same job?

_____

_____

_____

_____

_____

5. How much can you budget for each position?

_____

_____

_____

_____

6. Have you thought about the pay structure? If not, you need to do so. If you are thinking about the pay structure, briefly describe it for future reference.

_____

_____

_____

_____

_____

Below is a sample organizational chart tailored for a learning organization to showcase key positions:

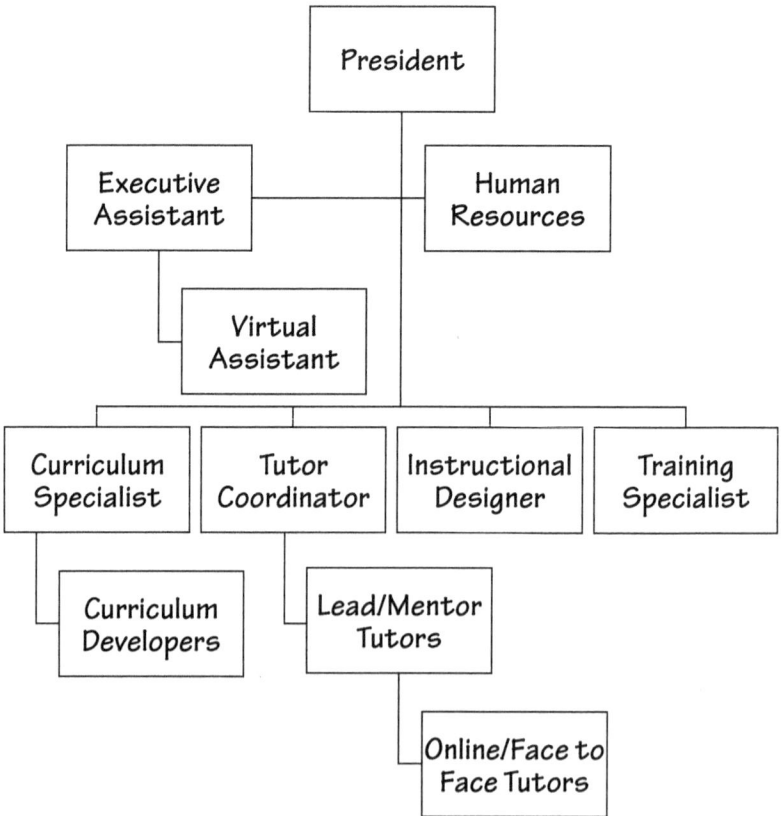

This is an organizational chart for any tutoring business that can be expanded for future growth.

Let's look at a brief description for each key position:

Key Position	Purpose
President	Manage the day-to-day operations. Strategic planning and business development. Final approval of payroll, final candidates, and other important tasks. Analyze and present research for to the board and appropriate employee and staff.
Executive Assistant	Manage any task designated from President. Primarily dealing with business affairs. Supervise virtual assistants. Write and prepare memos and other business communication.
Virtual Assistant	Manage any task related to the business. Social media tasks, managing emails, marketing efforts. Conduct research and market analysis.
Human Resources	Run payroll and manage taxes. Develop job descriptions and take care of hiring needs. Business insurances and liabilities. Background checks and performance reviews.

Key Position	Purpose
Curriculum Specialist	Manage curriculum projects. Develop and revise curriculum maps. Revise and update curriculum. Conduct research for best-practices and state of the art strategies. Works closely with instructional designers.
Curriculum Developers	Develop curriculum. Write content on a specific subject.
Tutor Coordinators	Review tutoring sessions on a weekly basis. Approve tutoring hours and send to payroll department. Schedule new tutoring assignments to tutors. Monitor and upload tutoring lessons in content library. Interview clients for tutoring services. Mentor tutors, when needed. Host tutor orientations and monitor monthly meetings.
Lead Tutor/ Mentor Tutor	Mentor tutors, when needed. Conduct mock tutoring sessions. Review tutoring sessions on a weekly basis. Conduct and host monthly virtual meetings. Report to tutor coordinator with concerns.

Key Position	Purpose
Online/Face to Face Tutors	Tutor diverse learners. Submit monitoring notes. Deliver engaging lessons. Develop lessons when necessary for additional pay.
Instructional Designer	Design tutoring lessons. Design professional development. Convert curriculum for web or print base. Work closely with Curriculum Specialist.
Training Specialist	Conduct all trainings. Manage professional development trainings. Schedule trainings. Send emails alerting professional development opportunities inside and outside of the learning organization. Manage Annual Professional Development Plans for tutors.

The bottom line is to realize that once your tutoring business has expanded there will be some key positions that will need to be filled by qualified applicants to run a successful learning organization.

Developing Job Descriptions and Pay Structures

Have you ever accepted a job and did not have clear guidelines on what is expected of you? Reflect on the unnecessary stress. Do you want that for your learning organization?

That's why job descriptions are important—they clearly outline the pay and expectations for a specific job assignment. In addition, they help individuals with professional development opportunities to refine their skills and continue to make positive contributions to the organization.

Developing job descriptions can be a task, especially if you do not know what you want. There are three strategies that can be used for developing job descriptions.

They are listed as the following:

Strategy #1	Strategy #2	Strategy #3
Look Online	Hire a Freelancer	Do-It-Yourself

Looking online requires you to search the Internet for similar job descriptions to get an idea of what is expected to attract talent to your organization. While this strategy seems easy, please keep in mind that most of these job descriptions are copyrighted and should not be copied at all. They can merely serve as an example for future descriptions you may write.

Depending on your budget, it may be a good idea to hire a freelancer specialized in HR or hire a HR company. They will have knowledge and skills necessary to design job positions that adhere to federal regulations and laws.

The last strategy is to develop the job description on your own. Honestly, you may have to do this so that you can get familiar about each key position within your learning organization. If you plan to take this route, it is very important to review federal laws and regulations to ensure that your descriptions are in compliance. If your budget permits, hire a freelancer to review your job description.

Below are eight questions that can help you develop your job description. Each of these questions can be used to draft a quality job description.

1. What are the physical demands?

    _____
    _____
    _____
    _____
    _____

2. What is the description of the work environment?

    _____
    _____
    _____
    _____
    _____

3. What is the required education and experience?

    _____
    _____
    _____
    _____
    _____

4. What are the required knowledge, skills, and abilities?

    _____
    _____
    _____
    _____
    _____

5. What is the overall position description?

_____
_____
_____
_____
_____

6. What are the areas of responsibility?

_____
_____
_____
_____
_____

7. How much does this position pay?

_____
_____
_____
_____
_____

8. What is the length of this position? What type of position is needed?

_____
_____
_____
_____
_____

Developing Pay Structures

Have you ever worked for a tutoring company that charged clients at least $60 per hour, but only paid you $10 an hour? You were grateful for the opportunity because it was extra cash coming into your pocket. Now that you are on the other side of the situation, what to pay your employees is much more complex.

Here are some questions that you should consider when developing pay structures for your employees.

1. How can I structure each position to provide pay increases based upon performance?

   _____

   _____

   _____

   _____

   _____

2. Is it a fair market rate? If not, what other perks do you have to set yourself apart from your competition?

   _____

   _____

   _____

   _____

   _____

3. Will this be included in the Employee Handbook or given as a separate document? Describe your reasons.

_____

_____

_____

_____

_____

4. How many positions can be considered independent contractors?

_____

_____

_____

_____

_____

5. How many are employee positions?

_____

_____

_____

_____

_____

6. What type of benefits will you offer to your employees?

_____

_____

_____

_____

_____

Let's look at a small tutoring business owner who provides online tutoring services.

Scenario 1:
"In the Fast-Lane to Digital Learning"

Ivory Beri, a former math teacher, decided that she wanted to follow her lifelong passion of helping students learn. After spending eight years in the classroom, she realized that she was making an impact on her students and made the bold decision to quit her full-time teaching job to pursue her dream. Since she discovered that students loved to learn online that is what she offered—online tutoring services for students in K-12 tutoring all subjects.

She developed a pay structure of the following:

Pay Structure	Pay Criteria
$13.00/hr	Currently in College
$14.00/hr	Associate Degree
$15.00/hr	Bachelor's Degree
$16.00/hr	Master's Degree
$17.00/hr	Doctorate Degree

This pay structure was designed this way because she was on a budget and only charged clients $35 per hour. Not to mention, the market value for tutors in that area was only $10 per hour. This pay structure would definitely attract talent. It's a good pay rate for someone who is working from home doing what they love to do—helping students.

Expert's Advice:

In the tutoring industry, there isn't a formula for developing pay structures. However, my goal is to at least give you an idea of what is fair when hiring help for your tutoring business.

Analyzing When to Outsource

There will come a time that will require you to outsource aspects of your tutoring business.

Here are some questions that you should ask regarding when to outsource:

1. How long will the project take? Do you have that kind of time?

   _____
   _____
   _____
   _____
   _____

2. What skill set is needed to complete the project?

   _____
   _____
   _____
   _____
   _____

3. What type of budget is available for this project?

_____

_____

_____

_____

_____

4. What additional resources are needed to complete the project?

_____

_____

_____

_____

_____

Each of these questions is important when it comes to outsourcing. Depending on where you post your projects, there may be a project template available to help you as well.

Expert's Advice:

When I started out as a private tutor, I did everything myself. This was mainly because my background was in curriculum development, educational writing, and instructional design. In my spare time, I would work for other private clients to develop online curricula. While your background may not be in the same fields, it is always a good idea to outsource some of your projects so that it will free up your time to do what you love.

Setting a Budget for Projects

Just like any other budget, you need to know what you want. Typical projects that tutoring businesses may need to be successful include a variety of projects, which may include a press release writer and so forth.

Let's look at a situation in which a tutor set a budget for her freelance project.

Scenario 2: "That's Too Much for Less!"

Shelly, an English tutor, decided that she wanted to hire a freelancer to design sixteen lessons for several clients. Her budget was between $250 and $500. Several freelancers placed bids that were over $500 and she had to decline them. However, there were a few qualified applicants that bid between $325 and $450.

Rather than going with the lowest bid, Shelly chose the best candidate with the knowledge, skills, flexibility, and experience to take on the position. She chose the bid for $380 that would be completed within six weeks. Although Shelly selected the best bid, she decided to contribute the entire $500 budget for this project. However, she only spent $380. After the six-week project ended, Shelly had $120 left for another small project in the curriculum budget category.

Expert's Advice:

Shelly did the right thing when she set the budget for this project. For future projects, she should use the same strategy to ensure that projects stay within budget.

Below is a chart to help you plan the type of projects you may need for your tutoring business. These projects include the following:

Types of Projects	Budget Categories	Budget Amount	Estimated Time Frame	Actual Amount Spent	Actual Time Frame
Press Release Writer	Marketing				
50 Lessons	Curriculum				
Contacting Customers	Admin Support				
Sales Copy for Educational Company	Marketing				
Corporate Identity Package	Creative Design				
Blog Identity Package	Creative Design				
Market Research in Education	Marketing				
Promotional Video	Marketing				
Content Writer	Content Writing				
25 Educational Articles	Content Writing				
Educational Special Report	Content Writing				
Tutor Handbook	Content Writing				
Algebra I Pre-Assessments	Curriculum				
Reading Assessments	Curriculum				
Website Design	Creative Design				
Membership Site	Creative Design				

This is a great way to look at projects to see where funds are going. It also gives you a tangible reminder of how projects are doing and which contractors completed each project.

As your tutoring business begins to expand, identifying what is needed and how to support a pay system that will be beneficial to all parties involved can be a challenge. Take the time now to effectively plan how you want your organizational chart and pay structures to function, especially when it comes to outsourcing projects. By using these strategies, you are destined to work with some of the best talent in the industries.

CHAPTER 4

Corporate Meetings and Minutes for Your Tutoring Business

"The reward of a thing well done, is to have done it."
—Ralph Waldo Emerson

Have you ever got lost without directions? I think that everyone has been lost a time or so trying to find a specific location. There are many reasons why this could have happened, but I am sure that a map or navigation system would have helped.

The same thing can happen with your tutoring business. It is very important to have some type of direction when trying to understand the next strategic step to take for your business. This is where both corporate meetings and minutes come into play.

Recognizing the Benefits of Corporate Meetings

You may wonder why it's important to have scheduled meetings for your tutoring business, especially if it is a Limited Liability Company (LLC).

The main reason is to protect your LLC status. Don't get upset; be happy about the additional paperwork. Let's look at the benefits of having corporate meetings.

Benefits of Corporate Meetings

Benefit #1: Be "In the Know"

While you may already know the direction in which you wish to take your business, you will have tangible evidence that business is booming and work is in progress.

Benefit #2: Gain Easy Access

If you plan to work with the government or apply for loans, you will need to provide a specific number (i.e. previous 6 months) of corporate meeting minutes. This is not always the case, but you will be prepared.

These are the main benefits of keeping corporate minutes. You will look back and appreciate them when you get in the practice of keeping them organized.

Preparing for Your First Corporate Meeting

You may or may not have a board of directors or multiple officers. However, your first corporate meeting should entail the following:

Creating Bylaws	Electing Officers

Setting a Corporate Meeting Schedule

Purpose of Bylaws

The purpose of bylaws is to establish how the business will be run and how often the board will meet for an annual meeting. If the President wanted to call a special meeting to address items stated on a board-approved agenda, the bylaws indicate the proper procedures for it.

Purpose of Electing Officers

You elect officers so that the business can operate and meet the status of being a corporation. You can expect to have the following types of officers: (a) President; (b) Vice President; (c) Secretary; and (d) Treasurer.

You may be saying that your tutoring business only has one person in charge—YOU. So, why would you need all of these officers? Please know that it is completely fine as your business is probably organized as a LLC.

These two tasks are enough for one meeting. However, you also need to select a meeting to meet at least once a month to discuss business affairs. If deemed necessary, another special meeting will need to be called to establish a corporate meeting schedule.

Developing a Corporate Meeting Schedule

While you may opt to have an annual meeting, it may be wise to have monthly assemblies in the form of regular or workshop meetings. A regular meeting focuses on the business topics that are discussed each month, while a workshop meeting focuses on developing a plan toward one or more topics.

While there is not a set formula for developing these types of schedules, individuals do need to keep in mind other important dates such as business meetings, conferences, and work schedules.

Here's an example of a corporate meeting schedule:

YOUR LOGO GOES HERE **[YEAR] Corporate Meeting Schedule**
<u>Type of Meeting Date Time</u> Regular Month, Day, Year Time of Meeting Workshop Month, Day, Year Time of Meeting Regular Month, Day, Year Time of Meeting Regular Month, Day, Year Time of Meeting Special Month, Day, Year Time of Meeting Closed Month, Day, Year Time of Meeting

Once your corporate meeting schedule has been established it is important to determine the type of information that should be included in corporate minutes.

Determining the Type of Information that should be Included in the Corporate Minutes

Corporate minutes are brief notes regarding topics discussed in corporate meetings. Just like the corporate schedule, there is not a set format on how to create these. However, there are some guidelines that you should follow. Let's look at the anatomy of corporate minutes.

The Anatomy of Corporate Minutes

When producing corporate minutes, the following elements should be made clear to protect your organizational structure status.

Elements of Corporate Minutes	Purpose
Type of Meeting	This will let stakeholders know what is expected in the meeting.
Purpose of the Meeting	This establishes the tone of the meeting and the focus of it.
Date, Location, and Time	All minutes need to have consistency and a sense of setting for verification purposes.
Old Business and/ or New Business	There can be a number of topics outlined in the minutes to support the corporate minutes.
Information about the Next Meeting	It's important to add information about the next meeting, which includes the "Type of Meeting, Setting details, including location."
Valid Authorized Signature	Corporate minutes will not be official until an authorized representative such as corporate officers can sign the minutes in ink. At that time, the minutes become official.

Setting Up a Binder System for Organizing Corporate Minutes

Organize your corporate minutes, including bylaws, in a binder for your learning organization. Use a 1- or 2-inch binder. It depends on the content for each corporate meeting. If the binder is being used exclusively for minutes, then you can store at least five or more years in there. If you are storing multiple years in this binder, then each section should be labeled accordingly.

Please see below:

SECTION 1   By Laws and Certificate of Formation

SECTION 2   Year 1

SECTION 3   Year 2

SECTION 4   Year 3

SECTION 5   Year 4

SECTION 6   Year 5

This is just one of the methods that can be used, but keep in mind that original signatures will need to be on file to validate the minutes.

In this chapter, you had the opportunity to look at why keeping corporate meetings is a good thing and how to develop a corporate meeting schedule. Also, you learned about the different elements that make up corporate meeting minutes and how to file them in an organized fashion.

CHAPTER 5

Planning Orientations for Your Learning Organization

Importance of Orientations in Your Tutoring Business

Orientations are important so that pertinent information can be shared with the specific audience. As you are planning how to educate others who may be doing business with your tutoring company or purchasing your services, you want to make sure that you explain to them the goal of the orientation. In this chapter, we will identify and describe the various type of orientation in which you will need to plan for your clients.

Parent Orientations	Student Orientations	Tutor Orientations

Identifying and Describing the Various Types of Orientations

The moment that you get a client, you will need to acclimate them how to gain access to your services. It is extremely important if you are tutoring online. Below are some questions to help you develop your in-take process look like.

Developing Parent Orientations

1. What does your in-take process look like?

_____

_____

_____

_____

_____

2. Are there any technology requirements? If so, what are they?

_____

_____

_____

_____

_____

3. How would you communicate available sessions and tutoring session lengths?

_____

_____

_____

_____

_____

4. What would be the recommended hours per week that you
    would recommend to parents?

    _____

    _____

    _____

    _____

    _____

5. How long would it take you to build or customize your cli-
    ent's tutoring program?

    _____

    _____

    _____

    _____

    _____

6. After the client's tutoring program is finalized, how do you
    plan on discussing the proposed student learning plan?

    _____

    _____

    _____

    _____

    _____

7. How do you plan on gaining parent approval of the student
    learning plan?

    _____

    _____

    _____

    _____

    _____

8. What are your pre-assessment directions? How would you communicate the pre-assessment process for your learning organizations?

_____

_____

_____

_____

_____

9. How would pre-assessment results be communicated?

_____

_____

_____

_____

_____

10. What can parents expect once the tutoring program has started?

_____

_____

_____

_____

_____

11. How does your welcome letter look?

_____

_____

_____

_____

_____

12. How do you plan on communicating attendance?

_____

_____

_____

_____

_____

13. What are the eligibility requirements for incentives in your tutoring program?

_____

_____

_____

_____

_____

14. What are your post-assessment processes? How would you communicate the post-assessment process for your learning organizations?

_____

_____

_____

_____

_____

15. What are your post-program requirements?

_____

_____

_____

_____

_____

16. How would you explain the need for both a child and parent survey?

_____

_____

_____

_____

_____

Describe the Students Orientations

Just like the parents, students need to be taught how your tutoring program works. That way they can be successful with their tutoring platform. Depending on how you want to share it, it is important to let the student's know about the parent's orientation. That way, everyone is on the same page.

Below are some questions to help you develop your own student orientation:

1.   What are you going to say in your welcome letter?

_____

_____

_____

_____

_____

2. What do you expect of the learners? (Please be sure to communicate these on a Kid-Friendly level).

_____

_____

_____

_____

_____

3. What are the technology requirements?

_____

_____

_____

_____

_____

4. How to participate in the classroom/tutoring session?

_____

_____

_____

_____

_____

5. How to take pre/post Assessments?

_____

_____

_____

_____

_____

5. How would you communicate the importance of attendance and effort?

_____

_____

_____

_____

_____

6. How would you communicate the purpose of progress monitoring assessments?

_____

_____

_____

_____

_____

7. How would you communication the eligibility of incentives or how to claim their incentive?

_____

_____

_____

_____

_____

8. What are the virtual classroom expectations?

_____

_____

_____

_____

_____

Describe the tutor orientations.

It is very important to have a tutor orientation. As you are developing your tutoring orientation, below are some questions to help develop your own tutor orientation:

1. How do you plan on introducing your own company to prospective tutors?

_____

_____

_____

_____

_____

2. What are the online tutoring hours and when do you expect tutors to be available for assignments?

_____

_____

_____

_____

_____

3. How do you plan on communicating the types of online tutoring assignments available?

_____

_____

_____

_____

_____

4. What state and federal laws will be covered and expected for tutors to follow?

_____

_____

_____

_____

5. What are the tutors' expectations in both face-to-face and online tutoring session?

_____

_____

_____

_____

_____

6. How would you explain tutor session reviews?

_____

_____

_____

_____

_____

7. How would you explain tutor performances and how will be assisted?

_____

_____

_____

_____

_____

8. How would you explain the professional development requirement for tutors?

_____

_____

_____

_____

_____

9. How will you communicate expectation for new online tutoring assignments?

_____

_____

_____

_____

_____

10. What is your policy for lesson plans and monitoring notes? How would you communicate that?

_____

_____

_____

_____

_____

11. How would you communicate where to submit required documentation?

_____

_____

_____

_____

_____

12. What are the mandatory requirements for tutors to get paid?

_____

_____

_____

_____

13. How do you plan on communicating information on direct deposit (i.e. payroll, timesheets, and pay dates?

_____

_____

_____

_____

_____

Expert's Advice:

The better the orientation, the better the tutors work. Make tutors sign off that they receive and understand the orientation. Follow up with tutor handbook.

Selecting the Best Platform for Delivering Orientation

When it comes to delivering orientations, it is important to keep the target audience in mind. It's very clear that we are in digital age, which means that technology is very important. However, organizational leaders may find that on-ground training is also important and serves a purpose. While I can't make the decision for you, but I can provide some thought provoking questions to help you make a solid decision on which platform for delivering orientation would work for your learning organization:

These questions are the following:

1. How do you plan on incorporating multimedia into your orientation?

_____

_____

_____

_____

_____

2. What role does technology play in your orientations? Is it major or minor? Why or Why not?

_____

_____

_____

_____

_____

3. How often do you update your orientations?

_____

_____

_____

_____

_____

4. How much are you spending to host orientations?

_____

_____

_____

_____

_____

Expert's Advice

When you are best starting out, you may option to have face-to-face orientations or have some sort of "free" option to host trainings. The most important thing that you need to consider is hosting trainings that are cost-effective and the best way to deliver the content. You may find that an online training is so much easier to manage and keep track of, which leads us to our next section. I will definitely share more pearls of wisdom in that section to help you make the best decision for delivering orientations.

CHAPTER 6

Developing Handbooks for Your Learning Organization

Identifying Your Handbook Needs

By now, you have probably realized that your tutoring business has grown and it is time to start documenting your processes, especially for hired help. Now is the time to spend a day planning out the various types of handbooks in which you may need. In this chapter, we will cover a variety of handbooks.

These handbooks are the following:

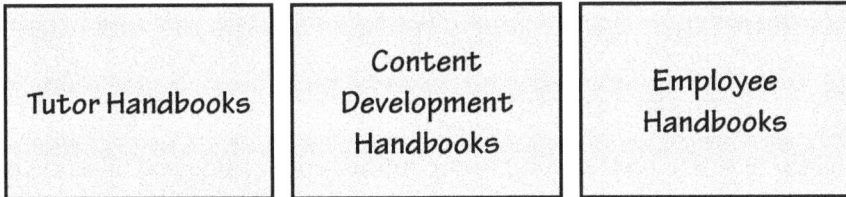

Tutor Handbooks	Content Development Handbooks	Employee Handbooks

On the next page are some questions to help you identify your handbook needs: Please write down your answers to the following questions. Your responses will guide you in identifying your handbook needs.

1. What types of handbooks do you need for your clients?

    _____

    _____

    _____

    _____

    _____

2. What types of handbooks do you need for employees?

    _____

    _____

    _____

    _____

    _____

3. What type of handbooks do you need for contractors?

    _____

    _____

    _____

    _____

    _____

These are three broad questions, but you should break it down according to the types of contractors and job positions in which you hire.

Developing a Strategic Plan for Writing Handbooks

Let's face it… you are busy person and you may not have time to flush out your handbook all on your own. Then again, you may have all the time in the world to work on your handbooks. Who knows?! Either way though, you will need to find at least

2 hours per day to make sure that you get your handbook ready to do the business. In my experience, I have recorded my notes and had my assistant to type it up. In other case, I have hand-written my notes and scanned them over for the assistant to type up. The bottom line is that you need to write your own hand-books specified to your tutoring business. I do have an online course on developing handbooks where you can get one-on-one support. To enroll in the course, you can send your request to support@thetutoroutreach.com.

Tutor Handbooks

When it comes to developing tutor handbooks, individuals need to be aware for what is expected of them. It's kind of hard to pin-point your exact policies, but I do have some reflective questions to help guide you in developing your handbooks.

1. How do you plan on communicating your learning organizations policy for accepting tutoring assignments?

    _____

    _____

    _____

    _____

2. How do you plan on having tutors share their contact information?

    _____

    _____

    _____

    _____

3. How do you plan on documenting attendance for tutors?

_____

_____

_____

_____

_____

4. How would you document your process for background checks?

_____

_____

_____

_____

_____

5. For some contracts in which you may get, how do you plan on communicating the finger print policy?

_____

_____

_____

_____

_____

6. How do you plan on communicating your learning organizations wait time policy?

_____

_____

_____

_____

_____

7. What is your policy for tutor timesheets?

_____

_____

_____

_____

_____

8. How do you plan on using final timesheet verifications? What would be the policy for submitting them?

_____

_____

_____

_____

_____

9. What is your policy for opening a tutoring session?

_____

_____

_____

_____

_____

10. What is your policy for closing a tutoring session?

_____

_____

_____

_____

11. What is your policy for submitting monitoring notes?

_____

_____

_____

_____

_____

12. What is your policy regarding assessments?

_____

_____

_____

_____

_____

13. What is your policy regarding lesson plans?

_____

_____

_____

_____

_____

14. What is your policy for communicating with your learning organization? Do you have specific email addresses dedicated? Why or Why not?

_____

_____

_____

_____

_____

15. How will you communicate what to expect and any policy related to how to handle communication from your learning organization?

_____

_____

_____

_____

_____

16. What is your policy on conducting a high quality tutoring session?

_____

_____

_____

_____

_____

17. What is your policy for dealing with at-risk students in tutoring sessions?

_____

_____

_____

_____

_____

18. What is your policy for dealing with gifted students in tutoring sessions?

_____

_____

_____

_____

_____

19. What is your policy for dealing with special needs learners in tutoring sessions?

_____

_____

_____

_____

_____

20. What is your policy on how to handle discipline in tutoring sessions?

_____

_____

_____

_____

_____

21. What is your policy on handling feedback from students?

_____

_____

_____

_____

_____

22. What is your policy for handling tutoring assignment limitations?

_____
_____
_____
_____
_____

23. What is your policy for inactive tutors?

_____
_____
_____
_____
_____

24. What is your policy for the length of sessions? Can sessions end early or late? Why or Why not?

_____
_____
_____
_____
_____

25. What is your policy for tutoring session overage?

_____
_____
_____
_____
_____

26. What are the technology requirements for tutors?

_____

_____

_____

_____

_____

27. What is the policy for email address?

_____

_____

_____

_____

_____

28. What is the policy on professional development?

_____

_____

_____

_____

_____

These are just some of the questions to help you get started. There's a great deal of more items that will need to be covered and we have more in detail in our online courses.

Content Development Handbooks

You will be writing your own content and will need to protect it. Let's face it you won't have all the time to develop your own lessons on other content that will need to be created to ensure that knowledge is being share with both clients and hired staff.

In the third book of my *Expanding Your Tutoring Business Book Series*, I go more in detail on how to protect your learning organization. As you are thinking about your content development needs, here are some reflective questions to help you create your own content development handbook. These questions are the following:

1. What are the copyright guidelines that you will include for content writers?

   _____

   _____

   _____

   _____

   _____

2. How would you explain the content writer's role?

   _____

   _____

   _____

   _____

   _____

3. What are the required writer qualifications for contracts that will be offered in your learning organization?

   _____

   _____

   _____

   _____

   _____

4. What are the steps for becoming a qualified content writer at your learning organization?

_____

_____

_____

_____

_____

5. What is the legal tax status for content writers in your learning organization?

_____

_____

_____

_____

_____

6. How do you plan on paying content writers? How long will it take to review their work?

_____

_____

_____

_____

_____

7. What does your course development and review process look like?

_____

_____

_____

_____

8. How will you communicate your course development and review process to writers and potential clients?

_____

_____

_____

_____

_____

9. What are the course standards or content standards?

_____

_____

_____

_____

_____

10. How do you plan on communicating confidentiality and non-disclosure agreements?

_____

_____

_____

_____

_____

11. How would you describe content writing opportunities?

_____

_____

_____

_____

12. How do you plan on communicating the proper legal forms required prior to starting a job?

_____

_____

_____

_____

_____

13. What are your sample project agreements?

_____

_____

_____

_____

_____

14. How would you describe your invoicing process?

_____

_____

_____

_____

_____

15. Will you offer bonuses for meeting deadlines? Why or Why not?

_____

_____

_____

_____

_____

16. How do you plan on communicating the process for qualifying for bonuses?

_____

_____

_____

_____

_____

17. What does your certification and release form for content or curriculum look like?

_____

_____

_____

_____

_____

18. Do you plan on having a course development rubric? Why or Why not? If so, what are the criteria?

_____

_____

_____

_____

_____

19. What are the roles and responsibilities of the content development and review team?

_____

_____

_____

_____

20. What are the instructional media guidelines?

_____

_____

_____

_____

_____

Describe Employee Handbook

You may not be at the point where you are ready to offer benefits to your employees. However, it does not hurt to start thinking about it. There are many different samples of writing an employee handbook, but your best bet is to check with the U.S. Small Business Administration. The bottom line is that an employee handbook is an important communication tool between you and your employees. Below are some topics that you should read more upon and plan accordingly for your own learning organization:

- ✍ *Confidentiality and Non-Disclosure Agreement (NDAS)
- ✍ *Conflict of Interest Statements
- ✍ *Equal Employment Opportunity Laws
- ✍ *Americans with Disabilities Act
- ✍ *Compensation
- ✍ *Standards of Conduct
- ✍ *Wage and Hour Laws
- ✍ *General Employment Info.
- ✍ *Employment Taxes
- ✍ *Safety-in-Security
- ✍ *Workers' Compensation
- ✍ *Computers-in-Technology
- ✍ *Work Schedules

- ✍ *Media Relations
- ✍ *Employee Benefits
- ✍ *Leave Policies
- ✍ *Optional Benefits

Expert's Advice

Yes, this is a lot, but you are setting yourself up for success. You want to make sure that you are legally preparing yourself to do business. Often times, government contracts will require that this information be on file. If you are just starting out, then you may be the only employee and that's fine. You may decide to hire a few contractors to help you get started until your business grows. Even then, you will need to be knowledgeable about the federal and state laws regarding hiring contractors. I go in more details about this in my second book of the Expanding Your Tutoring Business Book Series. This title is the following: Expanding Your Tutoring Business: The Blueprint for Hiring Tutors and Independent contractors. Hiring In my experience, I find that many miscommunications and understandings will be minimized by having well-written documentation. Also, you may want to consider having a signature page to have on file that they acknowledge and understand what is expected of them. Lastly, please make sure that organizational leaders are well versed in all handbooks. These should be referenced in meetings as well because you know how the old saying goes: "Out of Sight, Out of Mind" and you don't want that.

Selecting the Best Platform for Delivering Handbooks

The best platform for delivering handbooks will depend upon your preferences. Naturally, I am going to recommend providing an option for a hard-copy, but also host the handbook on the intranet or place where employees can have a designated place to refer back to it. You can also encourage them to print a copy as well. In either case, you need to have them sign a hard copy and scan and/or fax back to you, along with mailing a snail mail copy for company records. At the end of the day, it's your call to make this executive decision for your own learning organizations.

Copyrighting Your Handbook: Why it is Important?

You will be administering your handbook to hundreds and even thousands of individuals and you want to make sure that your work is protected. Therefore, it is important to take the time out now and invest in one's future. You may want to copyright under both your name and the learning organization's name to ensure that you will have a voice in the future.

Copyrighting your handbook is extremely important because it is considered intellectual property that is extremely attractive to prospecting buyers, if you plan on taking the route or even licensing your content to be used by other learning organizations.

CHAPTER 7

Listening to the People Who Matters

At some point, you may discover that you need to write down all the positive feedback or any feedback for that matter regarding your services and produces. In this chapter, we will look at creating surveys that will improve services, products, and your overall learning organization.

Why Surveys Are Important?

Surveys are important because one can use these to keep track of responses and actually analyze the data. There are great deals of surveys to utilize for your learning organization, which include the following:

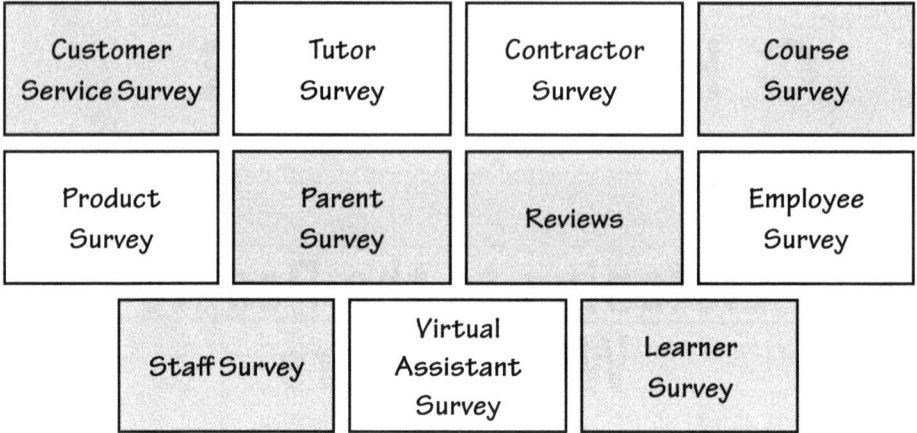

Customer Service Survey	Tutor Survey	Contractor Survey	Course Survey
Product Survey	Parent Survey	Reviews	Employee Survey
	Staff Survey	Virtual Assistant Survey	Learner Survey

Customer Service Surveys

The first type of survey that we will discuss is the customer service survey. This survey is so important because it provides feedback on how your customer service is, and can improve customer relations and overall company image.

Below are some reflective questions to help guide you in developing your customer services survey:

1. How long do you want customers to spend taking the survey?

_____

_____

_____

_____

_____

2. What is the timeframe in which the survey should be com-
    pleted and made available before the survey expires?

    _____

    _____

    _____

    _____

    _____

3. What is your strategy to remind clients to take the survey?
    How would this look?

    _____

    _____

    _____

    _____

    _____

4. What type of question could you ask about the visit?

    _____

    _____

    _____

    _____

    _____

5. Would it be important to know if it was the clients first
    visit? Why or why not?

    _____

    _____

    _____

    _____

    _____

6. What type of question would you ask to capture the nature or primary type of service that were provided on the specific visit?

_____

_____

_____

_____

_____

7. Would you use a rating system (i.e. scale of 1-5)? Why or Why not?

_____

_____

_____

_____

_____

8. How would you find out whether the staff or services provider was friendly, knowledgeable and courteous?

_____

_____

_____

_____

_____

9. How do you find out if the in-take process went smoothly?

_____

_____

_____

_____

10. How do you plan on allowing clients to add their own comment about your services?

_____

_____

_____

_____

_____

11. How do you plan on finding out how likely your clients will recommend your learning organization to others?

_____

_____

_____

_____

_____

12. How can you inform your clients about other services/produces on the survey?

_____

_____

_____

_____

_____

14. What will be your survey introduction that clients will see?

_____

_____

_____

_____

15. What would be your survey closure that clients will see?

_____

_____

_____

_____

_____

These are just some of the questions to help you get started. The biggest take-a-way is making sure that you have an idea of what you want to know about your learning organization business operations.

Expert's Advice:

If you provide a variety of services, then you will need to match each customer services survey to the appropriate service/product. For starters, you may want to brainstorm how you will keep track of all of this rich data.

Course Surveys

The next groups of people that you should listen to are students who may take your online courses or live courses. You may have taken a course survey before if you took any type of class in your career. When it comes to designing a course survey, you need to have an idea of the types of information in which you needed to collect data.

On the next page, there are some reflective questions to help you get started with your course survey.

1. What would be your survey introduction?

    _____

    _____

    _____

    _____

    _____

2. How do you plan on gathering feedback about assessments supporting the topics and objectives that were presented in the course or training?

    _____

    _____

    _____

    _____

    _____

3. How do you plan on gathering feedback about assessments supporting the course objectives and students learning outcomes?

    _____

    _____

    _____

    _____

    _____

4. How would you rate the instructor for the course or training?

    _____

    _____

    _____

    _____

    _____

5. How would you gather information on the learning environment?

_____

_____

_____

_____

_____

6. How do you plan on allowing students to share any feedback that they may want to share?

_____

_____

_____

_____

_____

7. How would you have asked about their preparation for the course?

_____

_____

_____

_____

_____

8. How would you close out the survey and thank the client for completing the survey?

_____

_____

_____

_____

_____

Just like you want to get feedback from clients and tutors, you also want to get feedback from clients who may be taking one or more of your courses/trainings.

Below are some reflective questions to help you get started:

1. How do you plan on keeping track of the courses on which are being evaluated?

    _____

    _____

    _____

    _____

    _____

2. How do you plan on linking the instructor's name to each survey?

    _____

    _____

    _____

    _____

    _____

3. What type of questions or insights would you like to know about the instructor? (i.e. communication, feedback, content knowledge).

    _____

    _____

    _____

    _____

4. Would you consider having learners complete a self-assessment regarding their relationship to the course and related materials? Why or Why not?

_____

_____

_____

_____

_____

5. If you do make the decision to include a self-assessment, how would it look?

_____

_____

_____

_____

_____

6. What type of questions or insights would you like to know about the course? (i.e. total hours spent, workload, address students' needs, class discussions, reading/resources, assignment and etc.)

_____

_____

_____

_____

_____

7. What type of question or insights would you like to know about the technical aspect of the course? (i.e. easy to access, course grade book, online tech. usage and etc.)

_____

_____

_____

_____

_____

8. What type of open-ended questions will you ask to see how the learning organization can improve?

_____

_____

_____

_____

_____

9. How does the learning organization do well?

_____

_____

_____

_____

_____

10. How the learning organization does the overall learning experience?

_____

_____

_____

_____

_____

Now, let's look at the reflective questions for bringing both a parent survey and the learner survey.

Parent and Learner Surveys

Parents surveys are importance because they will help you better understand the intake process and share information that may not be captured in an actual tutoring session. Below are some reflective questions to help you get started with your parents for your tutoring program:

1. How would you gather information about the intake process for your tutoring program?

    _____

    _____

    _____

    _____

    _____

2. How would you gather information about the detailed progress reports each month for your tutoring client?

    _____

    _____

    _____

    _____

    _____

3. How would you recommend or ask for a recommendation for your tutoring program?

    _____

    _____

    _____

    _____

    _____

4. How would you ask whether the tutoring program was beneficial to the learner?

_____

_____

_____

_____

_____

5. How do you plan on allowing parents and/or learners share additional comments?

_____

_____

_____

_____

_____

6. How do you plan on finding out whether the learner's grade improved, resolved a particular learning need, met learning goals, and increase the learner's confidence?

_____

_____

_____

_____

_____

7. How would you gather information about additional noticeable changes did you see in their child after participating in your tutoring program?

_____

_____

_____

_____

Now, let's take a look at how you can gain insight about the learner's experience in the actual tutoring sessions. Below are some reflective questions that you can answer to get the responses in which you seek:

1. How can you gather information about how the tutor explained the concepts in a clear way?

    _____

    _____

    _____

    _____

    _____

2. How can you gather information about how the tutor explained what the learner was learning before starting each tutoring session?

    _____

    _____

    _____

    _____

    _____

3. How can you gather information about the tutoring sessions starting and ending on time?

    _____

    _____

    _____

    _____

    _____

4. How can you gather information about how the tutor helped set goals for future tutoring sessions and the progress towards those goals?

    _____

    _____

    _____

    _____

    _____

5. How would you gather information about whether the learning was comfortable with the tutor's personality and communication style?

    _____

    _____

    _____

    _____

    _____

6. How would you gather information about whether the tutor suggested learning strategies that were helpful in learning the concepts?

    _____

    _____

    _____

    _____

    _____

7. How would you gather information about whether the learner had a better understanding of the concepts as a result of receiving tutoring sessions from your learning organization?

_____

_____

_____

_____

_____

8. How would you gather information about whether the tutor involved the learner in the tutoring sessions?

_____

_____

_____

_____

_____

9. How would you find out about the tutoring environment?

_____

_____

_____

_____

_____

10. Do you think that it is important to ask for the learner's recommendation regarding your tutoring program? Why or Why not? How would you know this?

_____

_____

_____

_____

_____

11. How do you plan on allowing learners share additional comments?

_____

_____

_____

_____

_____

I hope that those questions help you create your parent and learner surveys for your tutoring program.

When it comes to evaluating organizational practices with staff and contractors, it is best to link the survey to the organization and tasks. That way, your team can assess and make changes for future projects to run more smoothly.

Reviews and Customer Feedback

Most reviews are linked to product or services so that can be considered your product survey. There are a variety of places for your clients to leave feedback and/or reviews. It can be a scary thing because this is an area where you cannot control directly. However, you do have indirect control over the type of feedback that is left in the review. This is by doing everything that you said you would do. In other words, focus on quality rather than quantity.

Let's look at a few scenarios regarding reviews.

Scenario 1: "Fresh Off the Service "

Morris needed a curriculum developed for his upcoming book tour. He hired Jane's Tutoring Galore Company because her company offered tutoring and curriculum development as a service. About 3 week later, Morris had the curriculum and other resources that he had ordered. When he saw the curriculum, he was very excited about the work. He praised Jane's Team and immediately Jane asked him to share all of this in a review. Morris used the company's computer that was designated for clients to complete the review on an online review site. Just like you want to get feedback from clients and tutors, you also want to get feedback from clients who may be taking one or more of your courses/trainings.

Reflection: What Would You Do?

1. If you were in the same position as Jane, how would you have handed this situation?

    _____

    _____

    _____

    _____

    _____

2. After seeing the client's review, how could Jane respond to the online review?

_____

_____

_____

_____

_____

3. Do you think that it is necessary to respond to a review? Why or Why not?

_____

_____

_____

_____

_____

Expert's Advice:

Jane did the right thing to request, that the satisfied client publicized the good work that is going on at her company. This is a good way to gain business on other areas that the business offers.

It is important to know that the clients will leave reviews and/or feedback on their own. Whether it is positive, neutral, or negative feedback, you need to be prepared to respond in a fashion that is not defensive, but solution – oriented. In other words, if there is a problem, offer a solution. On some cases, there will not be a resolution, but is it important to not lost sight of your learning organization's mission.

Staff Surveys

Depending on how you got your business set up, you may need to have a variety of surveys or you may decide to have one survey with different categories. For instance, you may have a department for tutoring, contractors and core faculty. Depending on their roles and responsibilities, you may be able to determine the process. For surveys, you can reflect upon these questions:

1. How will you find out if the job responsibilities and deliverables meet expectations?

   _____

   _____

   _____

   _____

   _____

2. What do you want to know about the operations and procedures related to the specific staff position on a particular project?

   _____

   _____

   _____

   _____

   _____

3. How do you plan on using this information to lead your department or learning organization?

   _____

   _____

   _____

   _____

   _____

Expert's Advice:

It is very important to use these staff surveys to improve how you do business with your staff and to improve communication and working relationships with your staff. We don't live in a perfect world so, at times, you may receive some constructive feedback. However, it should be used to improve. Each day is a gift and there are many blessings and lessons to be had. There's not any difference in business. It's all about your mindset in how you view situations. Challenges are opportunities to grow so embrace all feedback from clients and staff.

CHAPTER 8

Giving Back to the Community

What is your definition of community? You probably learned in grade school that you were a community helper or inspired to be one. Without community, we lose a sense of purpose and coming together to make this World a better place. Let's face it...there was a community helper that helped you at some point in your life.

Community helpers that go above and beyond are considered Merchants of Hope. Before you read this chapter, think about the Merchants of Hope in your life back then and even now. Write down the names of these individuals here and write a brief sentence about how they helped you and why you considered them your Merchant of Hope.

Self-Reflection: Identifying the Merchants of Hope in Your Life

Merchant of Hope #1: _____

How This Person Helped You: _____

_____

_____

_____

_____

_____

_____

_____

_____

_____

_____

_____

_____

_____

Why You Consider this Person to be your Merchant of Hope?

_____

_____

_____

_____

_____

_____

_____

_____

_____

_____

_____

_____

_____

_____

_____

_____

_____

Merchant of Hope #2: _____

How This Person Helped You: _____

_____

_____

_____

_____

_____

_____

_____

_____

_____

_____

_____

_____

_____

_____

_____

_____

_____

Why You Consider this Person to be your Merchant of Hope?

_____

_____

_____

_____

_____

_____

_____

_____

_____

_____

_____

_____

_____

_____

_____

_____

_____

_____

Merchant of Hope #3: _____

How This Person Helped You: _____

_____

_____

_____

_____

_____

_____

_____

_____

_____

_____

_____

_____

_____

_____

_____

_____

_____

Why You Consider this Person to be your Merchant of Hope?

_____

_____

_____

_____

_____

_____

_____

_____

_____

_____

_____

_____

_____

_____

_____

_____

_____

_____

If there are more than this, then please use the notes section in the back of this book to continue your reflection.

How did this exercise feel? This is what it is all about…being a blessing to others. In other words, you are blessed to be a blessing to others. In this chapter, we are going to look at several ways to give back to the community.

Identifying Your Community

You may think that you know your community, but giving back to your community goes far beyond your state and neighborhood. I want to share with you a story about a young distinguished professional named Linelle Destiny.

Linelle Destiny grew up in poverty and started a club for girls, called the Secret Sisters Club. Throughout her school journey, teachers and professors helped her realize her potential. She later became a community helper and served as a leader. She got engaged, married and had children. Linelle Destiny started working in the change in the Woman's Ministry. She collected elephants (not real ones) and made crystal jewelry. Linelle loved to cook and bake. When she gets time, she writes, researches, and speaks on topics related to self-help, management and spirituality. Her husband, Alvin, is an Engineer so they teach a robotics class at the church.

Expert's Advice

It's very clear that Linelle Destiny is involved in a lot of things. Let's look at the possible ways that Linelle Destiny can give back to her community.

*At-Risk Community	*Teaching
*Marriage Community	* Math Science
*Sisterhood	*Self-help Community

*Motherhood   *Robotics

*Jewelry-Making   *Middle School & High School

*Spirituality   *College Community

*Business   *Culinary Arts Community (At-Home)

*Researcher   *Hometown Community

*Speaking Community

Do you see how we took all of Destiny's Experiences and identified the various communities? You have a great deal of communities as well. There are plenty of opportunities that must be considered when you make a decision to give back to the communities who gave to you. There's nothing greater than giving back from the heart. Remember, it is the flow of the heart that truly matters.

Now, just like Destiny, it's your turn to identify your communities.

Self-Reflection: Identifying Your Communities to Serve

_____

_____

_____

_____

_____

As a way to help you get started, here's some questions to help you get started:

1. How Do You Identify with this Community?

_____

_____

_____

_____

_____

2. How does your contribution impact this community?

    _____

    _____

    _____

    _____

    _____

3. What is the significance of this community to others?

    _____

    _____

    _____

    _____

    _____

4. Whom are some key contacts (and contact info) that can help you planning out your philosophy effort?

    _____

    _____

    _____

    _____

    _____

5. What is the time frame in which you plan on making contact with them?

    _____

    _____

    _____

    _____

    _____

Developing Scholarship Programs

Chances are, you may have received a scholarship towards your academic journey. How did it make you feel? If you did not get a scholarship opportunity for one reason or another then don't you wish that you had an opportunity? At first, you may not be able to give back because you are just getting started and is boot-strapped for cash. Don't worry---you can definitely give back in other ways and work towards a plan to give out scholarships. It's important to know that there is more about giving out scholarships than the fancy name that is attached to it.

Below are some reflective questions that will help you jumpstart your plans for developing a scholarship program:

1. How would you introduce your scholarship?

_____

_____

_____

_____

_____

2. How would you introduce your learning organizations to prospective scholarship recipients?

_____

_____

_____

_____

_____

3. What is your targeted audience for the scholarship?

_____

_____

_____

_____

_____

4. Why did you decide to offer this scholarship? In other words, what was the inspiration behind it?

_____

_____

_____

_____

_____

5. What type of application deadline do you plan on implementing for this scholarship?

_____

_____

_____

_____

_____

6. Will your scholarship be local, national or international? How will you communicate this to prospective scholarship recipients?

_____

_____

_____

_____

_____

7. How will the scholarship be administered?

_____

_____

_____

_____

_____

8. How many scholarships will be offered during a program cycle?

_____

_____

_____

_____

_____

9. What are the eligibility requirements for this scholarship?

_____

_____

_____

_____

_____

10. How do you plan on establishing a program cycle? How will this look?

_____

_____

_____

_____

_____

11. Describe your scholarship in one-paragraph.

_____

_____

_____

_____

_____

12. What are some F.A.Q.S that you can think of, that may need additional clarifications?

_____

_____

_____

_____

_____

13. What are the restrictions or limitations that scholarship applicants should be aware of?

_____

_____

_____

_____

_____

14. How do you plan on having prospective scholarship applicants? Submit an application package.

_____

_____

_____

_____

15. What are the requirements that should be included in the scholarship applicant application package?

_____

_____

_____

_____

_____

16. Would you allow applicants to submit a paper application or an electronic application package? Why or Why not?

_____

_____

_____

_____

_____

17. What does your learning organization look for when selecting recipients?

_____

_____

_____

_____

_____

18. Are you offering achievement-based or need-based? Why? Or Why not?

_____

_____

_____

_____

_____

19. How will you support prospective applicants for applicants looking for additional scholarship search resources?

_____

_____

_____

_____

_____

20. What contact information will you provide to find out more about the scholarship?

_____

_____

_____

_____

_____

21. Do you plan on having a scholarship committee to help make selections for quality purposes? Why or Why not?

_____

_____

_____

_____

_____

These are some questions to help you get started with developing your scholarship for your learning organization.

Becoming a Guest Speaker

Many learning organizations are looking for quality guest speakers who are willing, ready and able to serve humanity. As a guest speaker, you are able to provide keynote messages, motivational talks or vital information on a particular subject. Not only will these opportunities help the community, it will also highlight your learning organization and increase speaking opportunities that can turn into another revenue stream in which you can donate your learning organizations scholarship fund or charity of your choice. Who knows, you just might be able to find anonymous donors because of your community involvement.

Giving Back with Sponsorships

Have you ever been sponsored for an event or trip? How did it feel? Sponsorships are great ways to help others and bring awareness to what your learning organization is all about. There are a couple of things that you need to keep in mind, which are the following:

Things To Keep in Mind
Determine Your Goals
Identify Businesses Who You Want to Approach
Determine the Need
Determine What You're Offering
Who is the Sponsorship Contact

When focusing on obtaining a sponsorship, think about these reflective questions:

1. What are you hoping to achieve with the sponsorship?

_____

_____

_____

_____

2. Identify 2-3 goals regarding this sponsorship.

_____

_____

_____

_____

_____

3. Who might have a motivation to support your cause?

_____

_____

_____

_____

_____

4. What are you seeking? What is the business seeking? (Cash, In-kind donations, volunteer work).

_____

_____

_____

_____

_____

5. Will you offer sponsorship levels? Why or Why not?

_____

_____

_____

_____

_____

6. What would be the criteria for those sponsorship levels?

_____

_____

_____

_____

_____

7. Who is the specific person you will be working with for the sponsorship?

_____

_____

_____

_____

_____

Now, let's take a look at Intro Workshops and Webinars.

Hosting Intro Workshops and Webinars

Another way to give back to the community is to host introductory workshops. Depending on your product and services offerings, you can center your workshops on them. Another strategy would be to focus on topics that would supplement your current offerings. Let's look at how a business owner did that.

Scenario: "Gone, but Not Forgotten."

Shannon just opened her tutoring business in a new part of town. Her current clientele drives to come see her for tutoring and a few of them works with Shannon in online tutoring sessions. Shannon has decided that she wants to grow her clientele but does not want to spend a great deal of money doing so. As a result, she decides to start hosting introductory

Scenario: "Gone, but Not Forgotten." (continued)

workshops at her office. After her first workshop, she gained two new clients. Shannon decided that she would stop hosting workshops until she needed more clients. Did Shannon make the right decisions? Why or Why not?

Expert's Advice

I think that Shannon had the slight idea about hosting introductory workshops, but the intent was not pure. What I mean by this is that Shannon should have thought about adding value to her clients and giving back to the community more than once. The value should be placed on the clients and the paying clients will come. Shannon should have brainstormed a menu and workshops that could be tested to ensure that attendees received a positive learning experience.

I want to share with you some tips on planning.

1. **Create 6-10 possible workshops:** When starting out with workshops, it is important to brainstorm titles that can be presented in either workshop or webinars. There are topics that should focus on all targeted audience. For instance, if you are offering tutoring services, then workshops should be geared towards both learners and their parents, if you serve both child and adult-learners.

2. **Set tentative dates for One Calendar Year:** This can be a bit tricky because you will need to find times and dates that would work for your targeted audience, along with yourself. This is where on-demand webinars may be more attractive.

3. **Collect Data from Your Clients:** Simply put, ask them what they want! This is an opportunity to see where they need support, as they give your ideas on the topics in which they need.

4. **Think Value, Not Charges:** People don't like to be sold. You need to be upfront if you are charging and give details on what those charges will entail (i.e. tuition only, materials and books included). As long as they know what they are signing up for, then you will get attendees whether you offer the workshop free or with fee. Who knows, you may decide to offer a certain fraction of your workshops for free or perhaps all of them will be free. That's the beauty of being an organizational leader. Just make sure it is for the client and not for you.

Developing a Volunteer Program

As you begin to expand your learning organization, you will begin to see a need to have a volunteer program. So, let's focus on how to develop a volunteer program. You may decide to start a non-profit or your learning organization may already be a non-profit. Either way, you will need a volunteering orientation. We are going to focus on reflective questions to think about to help you plan a volunteer program.

Below are the questions to help you get started:

1. What do you want volunteers to know?

_____

_____

_____

_____

2. Why do you need volunteers?

_____

_____

_____

_____

_____

3. How would volunteers serve in your learning organization?

_____

_____

_____

_____

_____

4. What would you say in your volunteers' welcome letter?

_____

_____

_____

_____

_____

5. What details would you share about your learning organization to help volunteers assess whether the volunteer opportunity is a good fit?

_____

_____

_____

_____

6. How would you communicate the value of each volunteer?

_____

_____

_____

_____

_____

7. Are you planning on having paid volunteer staff as well? Why or Why not?

_____

_____

_____

_____

_____

8. How would you differentiate roles and responsibilities for both paid volunteer staff and unpaid volunteer staff?

_____

_____

_____

_____

_____

9. How would you communicate the policies, including employee policies?

_____

_____

_____

_____

_____

10. What type of insurance and liability coverage would be needed to cover volunteers?

_____

_____

_____

_____

_____

11. How do you plan on recognizing volunteers for their service?

_____

_____

_____

_____

12. What are the job descriptions for the type of volunteering opportunities?

_____

_____

_____

_____

13. How do you plan on communicating volunteer opportunities?

_____

_____

_____

_____

These are just some questions to help you get started.

Where to Go From Here

You have the blueprint to get started, and you should be on the lookout for the next book in the *Expanding Your Tutoring Business*.

You can join our group at www.expandyourtutoringbusiness.com to gain exclusive content, reserve either group or personal tutor coaching sessions, network with like-minded tutors, and stay updated about various aspects of the tutoring industry.

Also, you can visit the Tutor Outreach Group for more support and upcoming events at www.tutoroutreach.com. If you have general questions, comments, or ideas, then email us at support@thetutoroutreach.com.

References

Holland, A. (2010). *Becoming a Better Tutor: A Data-Driven Approach to Tutoring.* Bloomington, IN: iUniverse.

Holland-Johnson, A. (2012). *Expanding Your Tutoring Business: The Blueprint for Building a Global Learning Organization (1st. Ed).* Round Rock, Texas: iGlobal Educational Services.

About The Author

D r. Alicia Holland is one of those rare people who can say she is an educator, professional tutor, instructional designer, curriculum developer, online professor, life coach, consultant, speaker, researcher, and author and mean it. She started her teaching career at the age of 20 and later earned her doctorate degree in Education from Nova Southeastern University in Ft. Lauderdale, Florida in 2010 at the age of 26. Her God-Given talents and skills have attracted clients such as school districts throughout the United States, state agencies, and other leading learning organizations, including in the private sector.

Dr. Holland consults with tutors and other learning organizations both large and small. Her tutoring blog for tutors has been online since 2010 and she coaches tutors around the world. Typically, she speaks at major conferences each year on topics in education, including tutoring. Dr. Holland is an online associate faculty member at Concordia University Portland where she teaches doctoral level organizational leadership and writing courses in the School of Education.

Also, Dr. Holland has held appointments as an online professor at Ashford University, American College of Education, and Everest Online where she served in the capacity of Internship Supervisor for Bilingual and English Language Learner Educators and taught various courses in Education, Life Skills and Critical Thinking. Additionally, at Capella University, in the Graduate School of Education, she taught various courses in Education and currently serves as a Dissertation Mentor for Doctoral Learners. Lastly, Dr. Holland teaches doctoral level research courses and serve as either Dissertation Chair or Committee Member at the University of Phoenix. Currently, she is serving as a Lead Area Faculty Chair in Research and was awarded and recognized as one of the 2016 Senior Research Fellows for her research on Meditation, Mindfulness, and Critical Thinking.

When Dr. Holland is not developing new content, tutoring, teaching, or consulting with her clients, you can usually find her sight-seeing and spending quality time with her family enjoying the Desert Sunrises and Sunsets.

You can also find more of her work at www.dr-holland.com. If you are interested in working with Dr. Alicia Holland, please contact her using the contact form at her website.

Index

P

Parents, accommodation of, 25–26
Partnerships, 6
Pay structures, 44–48
Payroll, budgeting, 14–15, 32
Personnel
  key positions, 36–41
Planning your business
  corporate meetings, 51–56
  human resource (HR) needs, 35–50
  office needs, 20–21
  office space and, 25–26
  vision and mission statement, 1–2
Post Office (PO) Box addresses, 23, 27
President, 39, 53
Professional development, 17, 32
Professional liability insurance, 15, 32

R

Reviews, 119

S

Sales and use tax, 14–15
Saving a percentage of income, 12
Schedule of corporate meetings, 53–54
Scholarship Programs, developing, 130-135
Security features, 31
Software, 10, 11, 14
Sole proprietorships, 6–7
Sponsorships, 136-138
Start-up needs and budget, 9–17
Structure of organization, 36–41
Surveys, 103-123
  course survey, 108-113
  customer service survey, 104-108
  learner survey, 114, 116-119
  parent survey, 114-116

Notes

Notes

Notes

Notes

Notes

Notes

Notes

Notes

Notes

Notes

Notes

www.ingramcontent.com/pod-product-compliance
Lightning Source LLC
Chambersburg PA
CBHW072006090426
42740CB00011B/2113